In the Middle

Non-Official Mediat

Bradford Peace Studies Papers: New Series No. 1

In the Middle

Non-Official Mediation in Violent Situations

Adam Curle

BERG

Leamington Spa / Hamburg / New York

Distributed exclusively in the US by

ST. MARTIN'S PRESS New York

First published in 1986 by
Berg Publishers Limited
24 Binswood Avenue, Leamington Spa, CV32 5SQ, UK
Schenefelder Landstr. 14K, 2000 Hamburg 55, West Germany
175 Fifth Avenue/Room 400, New York, NY 10010, USA

British Library Cataloguing in Publication Data

Curle, Adam
In the middle: non-official mediation in violent situations. — (Bradford peace studies papers. New series; no. 1)
1. Mediation, International
I. Title II. Series
303.6 JX4475

ISBN 0-85496-506-8

Library of Congress Cataloging-in-Publication Data

Curle, Adam.
In the middle.

(Bradford peace studies papers; new ser., no. 1)
Bibliography: p.
1. Mediation, International. 2. Mediation, International — Psychological aspects. I. Title. II. Series.
JX4475.C87 1987 341.5'2 86-23257
ISBN 0-85496-506-8 (pbk.)

Printed in Great Britain by Industrial Press (Coventry)

Contents

Introduction

These pages deal with just one of the many activities aiming to create, maintain or restore the state of harmonious, constructive cooperation and just living together that we call peace. I would distinguish three main strands, all equally necessary, of these activities. One comprises all that we do to establish and nurture social and economic systems that minimise the inequality and want that generate conflict. The second is to act by all available non-violent means (I stress non-violence because it is an illusion to hold that peace can come through violence although it may come through power) against dangerous, violent, aggressive and oppressive policies. The third is to bring about reconciliation between those who are in conflict.

I am concerned here with the third strand, which is itself divided between mediation (or conciliation which is usually used almost synonymously), negotiation and arbitration. *Mediation,* as I use the term, aims to remove often largely psychological obstacles that prevent hostile parties coming together for constructive *negotiation,* which is the process by which protagonists reach an agreement through discussion and bargaining. In *arbitration,* the protagonists agree to accept the judgement of a respected third party. Reconciliation is a less specific term implying the restoration of friendship, and could in many ways also be applied to mediation.

Most of what I have to say is based on direct experience of fairly large-scale violent conflict over the last two decades. During this period I have been actively involved in mediation for twelve years. I do not mean that I was, so to speak, in the field all the time. When I was not, however, and was getting on with my normal life, I was still on call and the issues of the conflict were always simmering on the back burner of my consciousness.

For two reasons I do not recount the actual narratives of this work. Firstly, two of the mediations I have been involved with, The India – Pakistan war of 1965 and the Nigerian civil war (the Biafran war) 1967–70, have already been comprehensively written up by Yarrow (1978). Secondly, because the main issues and the actors with whom I have been embroiled in the last fifteen years, are still alive. But I have of course made ample use of the lessons and have transcribed suitably disguised conversations that I hope convey the flavour of the task.

Throughout these pages I make a number of generalisations about behaviour, especially by leaders, in situations of violent conflict. I have sometimes been asked whether cultural differences and the misunderstandings to which they give rise, do not make great difficulties for peace making in general and mediation in particular. They certainly may do so, and it is important for mediators and negotiators to understand them as much as possible. But they seem to me to constitute little more than variations on patterns which are, in my experience, more or less universal. I therefore discuss these general patterns rather than the somewhat different ways in which they may be manifested in different cultures. These can be readily grasped by those who understand the general principles.

Much of the work has been carried out under the auspices of the Society of Friends (Quakers) and I feel privileged to have been an heir to their three-centuries-long tradition of peace making, and to have worked with and learned from so many of its great examplars, among whom I have especial gratitude and respect for Walter Martin, Roger Wilson and the late Mike Yarrow. I would not, however burden them with responsibility for what I have written; the views I have expressed and the conclusions I have drawn are a personal interpretation of what I have myself experienced, and the flaws and mistakes are all mine.

I begin by discussing the psychological and other factors that make peace making difficult. The next two sections deal with the principles of mediation and the practice of mediation. In the evaluation, the effects of mediation are considered and, finally, a short but important proposal for promoting mediation is presented. The more I have pondered on the nature of violent quarrels and on the means of bringing them to an end, the more I have become convinced that mediation could be developed as a sovereign remedy for the scourge of conflict. But we need to know more about it and to practice it more widely and more systematically.

Obstacles to Peace Making

When quarrels rise to a certain pitch of violence the difficulty of reaching a peaceful settlement seems to increase sharply. This applies, in my experience, both in war and in family or marital feuds. Certainly the shedding of blood in the former marks a steep escalation of anger, resentment and blind chauvinism that inhibit any moves towards peace. This is particularly tragic in those cases where both sides really want a negotiated settlement.

These violence-induced and -inducing attitudes tend rapidly to harden. Fantasies, orginally based on reality but rapidly soaring far beyond it, develop concerning the barbarous wickedness of the enemy, making it increasingly hard to end the conflict other than militarily. More and more, as a result, does the task of peace making become a psycholigical one of changing these distorted perceptions, and less one of dealing directly with the territorial or other issue that precipitated the strife. This, of course, remains an issue, probably very serious, but one that is certainly exacerbated and mytholigised beyond all reason. However, whereas there can obviously be no single resolution to the innumerable possible substantive occasions of war, and therefore few generalisations to be made, the psychological forces they generate follow a more regular pattern. It is on the latter, therefore, that we shall concentrate.

Of course in some ways the hatred and suspicion between groups at war (or for that matter of individuals bitterly breaking up a partnership) are quite understandable. In the former case, the leaders among the protagonists (the actual fighters often feel little animosity), usually have some cause for anger and mistrust for each other, and are in addition tense with the burden of responsibility; their feelings are inevitably explosive.

Nevertheless, when all allowances have been made, it is hard to avoid surprise at the frequent extravagance of emotion. Dislike becomes phobia; suspicion, paranoia. The enemy is seen as diabolical in his crafty malevolence and treachery. Any compromise he may offer or peace initiative he may launch is automatically rejected as a trick designed to deceive.

The feelings, naturally, are reciprocal. X thinks of Y what Y thinks of him; each considers himself as brave, honest and peace-loving, but forced to take up arms by the war mania of the other. If told that this is just what his opposite number says of him, he will be hurt and angry; how could anyone believe such pernicious nonsense?

This mirror image may not be universal, but it is very common. Would-be peace makers should be on the watch for it, as it is one of the major obstacles they will have to face. If each side feels itself to be wholly good while the other is wholly bad, there can be little use in attempting a settlement based at least partly, as all settlements must be, on tolerance and acceptance of the other's position.

This tendency automatically to think ill of the other side, suspecting their motives or mistrusting their overtures, has other negative implications for peace making. It means that all information is twisted to serve the ends of this ideology of suspicion, for so it becomes. Even the most placatory statement is a deceitful ruse to spread confusion or gain a propaganda advantage. Thus although a great deal of accurate information may be available, it is read through tinted lenses and falsely interpreted as an added verification of the completely negative view of the enemy. Moreover, to the side that makes the misinterpreted statement it is further proof of their belief that the other has no interest in a settlement. Either way, both sides end up by having the minimal understanding of their enemy's motives and intentions and so are unable to take advantage of opportunities for working towards the peace which they probably both desire. This further raises the temperature of anger and resentment, intensifying the mutual mistrust.

But why is it that these irrational feelings are so powerful? Here we have to look beyond the specific exigencies of conflict and into the more general elements of human nature. We appear to have a need to build a self-image, an ego, that serves a dual purpose; it enables us to think well of ourselves and it muffles any disturbing sense of guilt and inadequacy. This is not the place to debate the origins of these negative feelings and our longing to evade or subdue them; they have been recognised by all major systems of religion and depth psychology although their source has been differently identified. For what it is worth, I tend to agree with those who blame them on our failure fully to grasp, and so to develop, the amazing potential of our natural endowment. Hence our deep but nagging sense of loss and failure for which the ego is contrived to compensate.

This ego is built around whatever we feel demonstrates, firstly to ourselves and secondarily to others, our goodness, worth, competence, courage, sensitivity. But this is best done by *comparison with others.* Hence it is essentially competitive, and thus it is the source of much greed, envy and, when we are unsuccessful, hatred of those who oppose or surpass us.

Obviously some individuals are more free of ego-compulsion than others, but few are so free that it does not burgeon in times of great tension and anxiety, when the roots of life are shaken. This seems very true of leaders in decision-making positions in time of war. This should not be taken as criticism of the forty or so persons at this level with whom I have had dealings. With a few exceptions they have been well above average calibre in both intelligence and maturity. Nevertheless, their attitudes towards both their country and their foes reached, at times, a pitch of distortion that would in normal circumstances have seemed extraordinary.

A major reason for this phenomenon is that, especially for leaders and heads of state, the nation or other group such as a guerrilla force, becomes an extension of the ego. A person's self becomes identified with this other entity. This is not strange in itself; lesser mortals project their egos onto the committee they chair, the club of which they are president, the family of which they are head; but the identifications are less sharp because the issues are not so portentous. However, to identify oneself completely with a nation at war is to commit oneself completely to its success and to the downfall of its enemy. It is not a case of one's country right *or* wrong; one can *only* be right and the enemy can *only* be wrong. It is therefore also necessary for the enemy to be evil, treacherous, cowardly, despicable, etc., etc., and for one's own side to be pure of heart, chivalrous and peace-loving. Any suggestion to the contrary is an insult both to the cause and to those who represent it. Someone who seems not to share this passionate chauvinism is anathematised, a central problem for a mediator.

These violence-justifying and -supporting trends are

heightened by a related psychological mechanism. The disguised feelings of guilt and badness that lurk in the unconscious may be legitimately disposed of by projecting them outwards onto an acknowledged object of scorn and dislike; anyone attempting to invalidate this useful target for negative emotions is likely also to become their target.

To some extent this applies to most individuals, but leaders are in addition subject to the specific pressure of guilt over the lives being lost or shattered upon their orders. This can become an intolerable burden and so it is the enemy who becomes the villain whose malignity forces them to shed blood.

This slide into irrationality certainly tends to be encouraged by the media, which elevate hatred into a virtue and suspicion into patriotism, and denounce as treachery any attempt at objective analysis of the situation. The more rabid the leader's speeches, the more they are praised for firmness and realism. Thus their extremism is spirally heightened by the forces they have themselves stimulated.

Other factors can also contribute to the psychological strain imposed on leaders. They are isolated, their very power and authority a well-nigh impassable barrier between them and most other people. They may fear that their advisers are keeping the truth from them, either because they wish to conceal their own blunders, or because they hope to curry favour by concealing what is unpalatable. Still worse, their ministers or generals may be conspiring to overthrow them; assassination is a constant possibility and I have known leaders who never left their military headquarters where they were guarded by a contingent of their fellow tribesmen. This is fertile soil for fantansies of persecution.

There are further impediments to peace making in which there is a blending of the psychological factors we have been discussing and what might be thought of as the mythology of war, itself probably a crystallisation over the ages of habitual psychological reactions.

The first is an excessive fear of showing weakness. It is obvious that if, in any fight, one combatant shows signs of giving in or running away, the other will attack with renewed vigour. But in war, it is often taken to self-defeating lengths. Thus more often than not it is seen as weakness to offer or to respond positively to any conciliatory gesture, such as a proposal to exchange wounded prisoners. Those who have been involved in negotiating such a deal well know how fraught with difficulty the most trivial detail becomes. A related issue, but one that tends to be more personal to a particular leader, is that of face, which is a culturally conditioned way of expressing the ego, perhaps particularly significant in the East but very common everwhere. Great care is taken to avoid anything that could be seen as a climb-down or abandoment of principle; there must be no loss of face, even at the cost of things that might seem much more important.

One dangerous precept of the war mythology is: always negotiate from strength. In one way this also makes sense; the loser or probable loser won't be able to drive a good bargain, his vulnerability will be taken advantage of. But to adhere slavishly to the principle is a recipe for continual escalation and the story of most wars is, in fact, one of escalation. It works like this: side A, seeming to have a slight advantage, issues its terms for a settlement; side B, fearing to be put upon, attempts to rally and build up its forces so that it in turn can impose terms on A; of course A will, for the same reason, refuse them, and try to regain its lost advantage; and so on until one or even both are exhausted or crushed.

In any case, however, policy is all too often based on illusions about the strength and intentions of the enemy. In consequence, promising possibilities for a settlement, greatly desired by both sides, have been lost. I would argue that, whatever the circumstances and however discouraging the conventional military wisdom, it is almost always sensible, and not a sign of weakness, to accept a proposal to negotiate, either on a specific issue such as a local cease-fire, or a general settlement. It may often, on the contrary, be a sign of strength. The risk is slight, for it turns out that the negotiation is simply a delaying tactic it can be broken off; and surely it shows courage and confidence to take a chance for the sake of possible peace. It would seem to be a much worse gamble to go on fighting in the certainty of continued death, destruction and suffering.

But although in many cases the protagonists would sooner be talking than fighting, both are trapped in a cycle of events from which they do not know how to escape. They would like to negotiate and often their respective demands are not impossibly incompatible. However, they are too suspicious of their enemies to trust them not to cheat, too firmly fettered by the shibboleths of warfare, too ignorant of the foe's real intentions and motives, too intent on maintaining an implacably tough self-image, too afraid of alienating their allies or influential supporters by any suggestion of giving ground: and their opposite numbers in the other camp are just the same. Consequently they either refuse to negotiate, or do so in such a hostile and tight-fisted manner that nothing comes of it. So the war goes on until one side collapses, or there is additional outside involvement, or some other circumstance that alters things. In the meantime, the misery will have continued; the peace which both sides had wanted all along will now be even harder to attain in any real sense because of increased anger, bitterness and confusion.

I am not, of course, suggesting that a satisfactory negotiation is always possible. The conflict of interests may be too great for compromise, or the demands of one side may be totally unacceptable to the other. Nevertheless, the obstacles to peace are very often more psychological than substantive. The purpose of mediation is to remove or reduce these obstacles.

Mediation

Mediators, as the word implies, are in the middle. This is true in two senses. Firstly they are neither on one side nor the other; secondly they are in the centre of the conflict, deeply involved in it because they are trying to find a satisfactory way out of it.

Although mediation is considered here in the special context of violent conflict, it is a universal human role. All of us, perhaps even the most intractably aggressive, have practised it occasionally. We may not have called it that when we tried to persuade members of our family or friends or colleagues to see each other's point of view and stop bickering about some trivial issue. But mediation it was: we were the people in between those who had fallen out, on fairly good terms with both, not taking sides though often pressured to do so; not personally implicated in the dispute, but worried about the situation and hoping to improve it.

What mediators do is to try to establish, or re-establish, sufficiently good communications between conflicting parties so that they can talk sensibly to each other without being blinded by such emotions as anger, fear and suspicion. This does not necessarily resolve the conflict; mediation has to be followed-up by skilled negotiation, usually directly between the protagonists, supported by a measure of mutual tolerance and by determination to reach agreement. But it is a good start.

This would apply whether the conflict were between individuals or nations, and irrespective of culture, political ideology, or religion. Although the circumstances of an international dispute, economic, political and strategic, are very different from the emotional tangle of, for example, a marital one, both ultimately focus on human beings who have to make decisions and to act, and whose passions, fears, hopes, rage and guilt are much the same whoever and wherever they are. This, at least, has been my experience.

Non-official mediation

Within the context of violent conflict, the forms of mediation may differ considerably. Some involve short-term missions having a very specific objective, such as those of Terry Waite to secure the release of captives in various parts of the world, or the shuttle diplomacy of a Henry Kissinger hurrying, often without great success, between one capital and another. There is also the longer-term work of United Nations officials such as Dag Hammarsjöld, Brian Urquhart or Sean McBride, struggling year after year to resolve one bitter quarrel after another.

These and many other patterns may be useful and appropriate. What I shall discuss is mediation usually of long duration, carried out by non-official groups or organisations, churches or other religious organisations, charitable bodies, academic bodies, or concerned individuals without institutional backing (although individuals without such support tend to experience difficulty in launching and maintaining their mission, suffer considerable strain and naturally incur considerable costs). I shall not speak of UN mediation, most valuable though it is; the aegis of a great international organisation creates conditions, occasionally less favourable where there is unilateral distrust of it, different from those pertaining to both governmental and to private or non-official mediation. What I have to say derives from direct experience of mediation initiated by the Quakers who, of the half dozen or so organisations I know of that have worked in the field, have the longest and most varied experience, as well as from efforts which were personal although carried out with much help from others.

It is perhaps hardly necessary to emphasise that those engaged in private mediation are never, so far as I know, paid, except for their expenses. Nor do they, being constrained by the need for confidentiality, make money or achieve any ego-enhancement by such means as writing articles or giving interviews. Their mediation is perhaps more appreciated because in no sense influenced by the profit motive; there is no reason why they should submit to considerable trouble and inconvenience except to contribute if possible to the reduction of human misery. In the same vein, I sometimes point out to people that I have been retired for several years and would sooner spend my old age at home than gallivanting around the world.

There are, of course, some disadvantages to non-official mediation. There is no automatic entrée, such as an ambassador would have, to recognised authority; there is no established source of intelligence information; there is no help in making appointments and travel arrangements, and with secretarial chores, all of which may be a considerable burden in some conditions; above all, there is no *power* such as would be enjoyed by the representatives of an important country who could reinforce arguments by a combination of threats and promises. Oran Young (1967, 1972) concluded that private intermediaries without political power and resources, lacked the 'saliency' to achieve major diplomatic results.

There is, however, one very considerable advantage. Paradoxically, it derives directly from the major disadvantage. The protagonists with whom mediators work soon discover, if the mediators act correctly, that their sole motivation is concern for the suffering occasioned to both sides by the conflict, and determination to do everything in their power to reduce it. They are not concerned with who wins or loses, they do not take sides, considering the only enemy to be war and the waste and suffering it brings; they are consistent in their honesty, concern and goodwill. Unlike official diplomats, however humane they may be, their aim is not to promote the policy of their own country; by contrast it is recognised that a country's official representative must carry out the instructions of the country he serves, even if they go against the best interests of the one to which he is accredited. Thus in certain respects the non-official or private mediator may be confided in and trusted more than the official. A futher advantage of the private position of mediators is that they may be disavowed if for some reason they cause embarrassment, or even expelled from the country without causing a diplomatic furore; they are both useful and expendable.

What then do these people do? First of all if, as may well happen, they are not already well known or have not been specifically invited in, they must get approval for a visit to the country or countries concerned and then gain acceptance from the people with whom they must work, preferably key members of the governments concerned — this process will be considered shortly. Their proper work, when it actually begins, is to open up better communications between the warring parties. This includes such tasks as taking messages from one side to the other, usually enlarging on the implications and the meanings behind the message; they do a considerable amount of explaining the motives and intentions of one side to the other; they interpret the statements or the cryptic 'smoke signals' sent up by either combatant; they correct wrong information and mistaken impressions obtained from statements and speeches by leaders of the other side; they attempt to identify the common interests of the protagonists; they make suggestions about how to improve communications between the protagonists and how to avoid obstacles to reaching a settlement; they try to establish friendly relations with as many people as possible, especially decision makers, on both sides; and they try to keep as well informed as possible about the situation so that they can speak about it constructively without making fools of themselves and so discrediting their ability to act in an informed and helpful fashion. In order to carry out these tasks they may often have to make difficult and even dangerous journeys, seek people out in remote camps, and suffer some of the discomforts and privations of wartime conditions. Although they hope for friendly relations with all concerned, they will probably also make enemies, for there are always some who do not want peace, the hawks who think that it would be possible to get a better deal by continuing to fight. A mediator who favours peace, especially if listened to sympathetically, may be a threat they would wish to dispose of.

We should also consider what mediators do not do and what they are not. They are not negotiators. Negotiators are concerned with the nature and details of any settlement being considered and with the bargaining by which it is achieved. They are usually representatives of the conflicing parties and so by no means impartial. Mediators, on the other hand, have no partisan view on the character of a resolution. By the same token they would consider it improper interference to promote their own solution; their job is to facilitate an acceptable one by helping to clear away obstacles of prejudice and misunderstanding that impede the protagonists in reaching an agreement together. This is not to say, of course, that mediators may not move between the negotiating parties trying to help maintain good communications.

Mediators should also be very cautious of involvement in conflicts in which one side obviously possesses far more power than the other and is genuinely confident of victory.

The reason is not that the weaker, and often oppressed, side should not be forsaken, but that mediation simply will not work. The strong are not going to heed any appeal for clemency or compromise. Why should they? They are confident that they can get what they want without giving an inch. If they do not reject the idea of mediation outright, they use the mediators to do their own dirty work by proposing terms to the weak which are tantamount to surrender; terms which, if accepted, would in many cases simply restore the conditions that led to war in the first place. Mediators can only make it clear that they will have no part in such trickery; their purpose is to work for a just and harmonious peace, not the passivity of subjugation. Submission at this stage without any resolution would in any case most probably be followed by a renewal of the conflict, for no situations are permanent.

What else can mediators do in such circumstances? Firstly, before they withdraw, they must ensure that their evaluation of affairs is really correct, that the strong are implacably obdurate, or that the weak have no chance of matching their power and so engaging in fair negotiations. Even if they decide they were in fact right, it could still be wise to try to build up relationships, perhaps with opposition leaders or significant non-official people, which could help initiate mediation when/if the situation eventally changed. For example, friendships made by some mediators with Zimbabwean African leaders several years beforehand greatly facilitated mediation when that became possible.

Mediators may possibly decide that they must temporarily abdicate that role and its impartiality to throw in their lot with the weak; this is purely a matter of personal conscience and judgement. However, if they do decide to serve the victims of violence directly, their best and most appropriate role may be to help empower them through understanding their situation more clearly, and organising and practising non-violent resistance. I might add that in different circumstances, rightly or wrongly, I have responded in all these ways.

Long-term mediation

A major feature of this sort of mediation is its long duration, running often into several years. Admittedly there have often been brief mediations, persuasive arguments brought to bear upon the parties in a quarrel that has suddenly flared up and which, when tempers have died down, is as speedily put right. More often, however, what seems superficially like a short mediation is only an incident, even if a crucial one, in a process that started before and will continue after it; such was the mediation that led to the Camp David agreement; there a process lasting days was preceded by a long preliminary period and is still in some senses going on.

The truth is that peace making of any sort *is* likely to be a very long process. The greatest virtues for mediators are hope and patience, for during the period they must stick with the intransigent problems of peace making endless obstacles arise, often when the prospects seemed brightest. Sudden changes on the battlefield, the replacement of a 'dove' by a 'hawk', some external intervention, a rumour, a tactical error, may all demolish months of painstaking preparation for a peace initiative.

But the work of mediation, by its very nature, can seldom be carried out speedily and for the very same reason that conflicts cannot be terminated speedily: they depend more upon human perceptions than on external circumstances, the former being more stubborn and hard to influence than the latter. In the slow move towards negotiation, settlement and the eventual restoration of fully peaceful relations, the significant stages are the changes of vision rather than the signing of agreements that result from them, the gradual erosion of fear, antipathy and suspicion, and the slow shift of public opinion. By contrast, the cessation of actual violence as a result of military victory may lead to a speedy settlement which usually is by no means peace in the sense of harmony and mutual regard. The victors dictate terms which cannot be refused, it is as simple as that.

It is therefore appropriate for mediation to be carried out by non-officials who do not run the risk of being transferred but who can remain with the job, consolidating the relationships on which all peace making depends and following the ramifications of the unfolding situation, the rise and fall of the various actors.

To become associated with such a mediation is to make a commitment to becoming an element in a scene of conflict for a significant period of time. Those I have been involved with have lasted up to four years and never less than two. My colleagues (when I had any) and I were not of course on the spot the whole time; I, for example, would return to my base at home or university and resume my usual activities of teaching and writing and being a husband and father. But the war is never far from the surface of thought, there are letters and telephone calls about it, many meetings in various places; the suitcase remains metaphorically and often literally packed. We keep in touch as closely as possible, debating the meanings of new developments, planning the strategy and timing of the next visit. As soon as we accept this role, we accept responsibility for playing a part in a terrible drama; and the part must go on, unless an understudy can be found, until the tragedy is over.

Beginning a mediation

It may be of interest to consider the ways in which mediation begins. Sometimes an organisation, or perhaps more likely an individual, is directly approached because of her/his reputation, and asked to mediate, perhaps on a very specific issue. S/he will then no doubt agree and go ahead with whatever support from her/his orangisation is available. Where there is not a direct approach the entrée is obviously more difficult. In my necessarily limited experience it may happen in a way that is either haphazard or on the contrary well planned. In one case I visited a scene of violent conflict because I was interested in what was happening. It was only after repeated visits that I found I had worked myself into a job, was known to and accepted by a number of people, and that my toing and froing between different groups appeared to be welcomed. So I continued for several years until circumstances made continued work less productive that it had been and I was asked to take part in a more urgent and at the same time more hopeful enterprise. But this kind of more or less solo effort is not often possible, if only for financial reasons.

A more organised effort also tends to begin with the concern of an individual for a particular situation which s/he then brings to, for example, the Quakers. Then (speaking only for the Quakers with whom I have been through the process several times) the sequence is likely to be something as follows.

The individual discusses the issue with the appropriate group within the Quaker organisation and a preliminary decision is reached. This might be to explore further; to say 'no' because it is impracticable (there might be no qualified person to undertake it) or it might have lower priority than other projects under consideration; it might be referred to another branch of the Society of Friends, possibly the Australian Quakers if it is a conflict in the Pacific area; or it might seem that the main need is for relief rather than diplomacy.

If, however, it is decided to examine the matter in greater detail, more people will be consulted. Visits will be paid to the local representatives of the parties concerned, to the Foreign and Commonwealth Office in London, the State Department in Washington, to the appropriate branches of the UN in New York and Geneva. The purpose of these visits will be to get further information on the situation; nothing will be said about mediation, because it would be premature to do so.

If these early enquiries appear to favour the possibility of eventual mediation, the next step might well be a reconnaissance. A small group of people will visit the ambassador(s) of the nation(s) involved to express their distress at the suffering caused by the conflict. They will ask if there would be any objection to visiting the country concerned to learn more about the situation, as their organisation feels that media reportage is inadequate. The usual response would be to welcome such a visit since it would 'enable you to see through the lies of our enemies'. It is the first demonstration of the mirror image that the representatives of each protagonist tends to make a similar observation, each implying that *they* are honest, peace-loving and truthful, while their foes are the opposite.

If all goes well, the reconnaissance team sets off. There will probably be two or three individuals: one is too few as the combined judgement of two or three is desirable; four is too many — they constitute a delegation to whom senior officials speechify rather than converse.

In general the team will find that people are only too willing to talk. It will have to listen, time after time, to almost identical recitals of the wrongs inflicted on them, and of the unrivalled barbarity and ruthlessness of their enemies.

But the transition from fact finding to mediating has yet to be made. The simplest crossing of the gap occurs when the team tell some senior person that they are going to visit the other side and ask 'is there anything we can do for you there?' The answer might be, 'I would be very interested in your impressions', of 'if you see so and so, you might say . . .' and perhaps a message of some slight significance may be given.

I have guessed that such responses are made as much to test the objectivity, impartiality and honesty of the team, as in the hope of learning anything useful. A friend and I met with a good example of this during the Nigerian civil war. At an early stage of our work, before we had met General Gowon, the head of the Nigerian military government, the Quakers had a tentative plan for a secret meeting of senior people on both sides. This, it was thought, could be more effective than previous efforts which had been spoiled by publicity. Such a proposal could be agreed to only by Gowon, but we had great difficulty in making an appointment. Various fairly senior officials tried to arrange one, but we were told that they were always vetoed by someone called Mr King, whom we imagined to be a white adviser, a sort of *eminence blanche* (in fact he turned out to be a Nigerian and became a close and valued friend). However, at length the permanent secretary of the Ministry of Foreign Affairs thought our idea was good, and overrode King. We had a meeting with the general, who was slightly interested in the proposal but doubtful over our proposed visit to Colonel Ojukwu, his enemy, the Biafran leader.

'He will simply use your visit for propaganda purposes', he said, 'claiming that the Quakers support his cause.' We assured him that we would give Ojukwu no cause to say that, and asked if he was actually asking us not to go. 'No,' he answered, 'but please don't say anything that could be taken to mean that you are going at my suggestion. It would be a dangerous mistake for him to think I was taking that sort of initiative. Moreover,' he continued, 'you will have to fly on one of the rebel pirate arms-carrying planes which my fighter aircraft have orders to shoot down. I am afraid I could not make any arrangements for the safety of your particular flight.' We assured him that we would be tactful in our dealings with Ojukwu and that we were prepared to risk the possible dangers of the flight. He then said: 'When you see him you might tell him that in the event of a cease fire agreement I shall order my troops to halt their advance and arrange for a neutral buffer force to safe-guard the cease fire'. This in fact was an advance on previous conditions. Gowon finally wished us well and said he would be very interested to hear of our experiences and impressions if we returned safely, which he hoped we would. We did, and were given an immediate appointment with the general, who greeted us very warmly. This was the beginning of a very good working relationship which lasted throughout the remaining years of the war.

This is how one mediation began. There had been a round of meetings and discussions at the UN in New York and at Washington, and there had been a reconnaissance lasting several weeks. But the real mediation did not start until we were given a specific message to deliver by General Gowon, returned with a response (not in fact an acceptance, but the idea remained alive) and, as was shown by monitorings of the Biafran radio, our visit had not been used to promote our own publicity or the Biafran cause. The fact that we had been prepared to face a certain amount of danger for no personal gain also counted considerably in our favour on both sides. After this the scope of our activities increased greatly in all the four categories of mediatory work which will be considered in the next section. I should add that in cases where extreme ideological differences are involved coupled with rigid stereotypes derived from them, the process of gaining acceptance may last much longer and be infinitely more complex.

Difficulties of mediators

We have discussed some of the intrinsic difficulties of peace making. To these must be added those peculiar to mediation.

The essence of these is that mediators are trying to bridge with friendship the hate-filled gulf between people who may well be killing each other and so generating the paranoid anger and suspicion that justify ghastly excesses. How can the protagonists trust these people who claim also to be on good terms with their sworn enemies? In fact it seems to be a tribute to the genuine desire for peace and essential good sense of most of the leaders I have met, that they were able to tolerate and even develop warm relations with such ambiguous characters.

It is certainly true, however, that mediators have to be constantly alert lest an unguarded word give any suggestion of favouritism of the other side. For example, to refer to Northern Ireland as Ulster to a Republican or as the Six Counties to a Loyalist would immediately put impartiality in question. Even the most tentative suggestion that one accepts the enemy's case, or their explanation of a particular happening, re-arouses suspicions that had been lulled by months of tactful and consistent good will. On two occasions in my experience during the Nigerian civil war (the Biafran war) other branches of the Quaker organisation concerned, not knowing of the mediation, issued statements implying sympathy with the starving Biafrans. Although the mediators had known nothing about this, a shadow was cast temporarily over their relations with the Nigerian leadership; if these relations had not already been very good, they would no doubt have been broken off. (On the subject of Biafra, to have referred to it as such would have been disastrous; we used instead the euphemism 'the other side')

Of course there is no question of concealing from one side one's relations with the other. This is central to mediation. If mediators did not inform X that they were going to visit Y who he hates, they might be spared some embarrassment, but they would be suspected of doing something even worse. If, moreover, they were caught in deception they could be thought of as spies or informers. In any case their usefulness as mediators would be over. No, it is best at all times to be honest and open. It is only by unswerving truthfulness, friendliness and concerned impartiality that mediators earn the conditional right to be on good terms with both sides.

But here let me interpolate another difficulty. Mediators must indeed be truthful if only because even the whitest of lies would, in this highly charged atmosphere, be a proof of mendacity. On the other hand, they must also be true to their principles; they are thought to be motivated by moral values rather than profit and hopes of advancement, but any lapse would throw doubt on their probity. They must, however, not only be truthful but tactful. These three demands upon them may sometimes come into conflict.

Suppose some atrocity is committed, are they to make no protest, in which case the sincerity of their principles will be questioned; or are they to say they are shocked and horrified, thus possibly seeming to imply sympathy with the enemy, and so giving grave offence? Perhaps the best approach is to express sorrow, but in a way that suggests no blame except to the practice of war, which makes such tragedies, committed by either side, inevitable. Faced with this dilemma, I have usually found that taking this line did not violate my conscience. If, however, atrocities are denied or attributed to the enemy with suspicious regularity, mediators must decide whether to risk a blazing row, or to remain pointedly silent.

In the early stages of their work, attempts may be made to use mediators in various ways. In particular the protagonists try to win them over to their side. This appears to be a fairly natural impulse of those engaged in conflict, but if successful, it would obviously subvert any efforts at real mediation. However, if leaders really want the possible fruits of mediation, they soon get the message and exchange the potential propaganda value of 'converting' the mediators for collaboration with them. There are also, however, more subtle ways in which mediators may be used. They may be asked to give messages that are intentionally misleading, suggesting, for example, that one side is eager for negotiations when it really hopes to lull the foe into a false sense of security, facilitating the preparation of new positions or the launching of a surprise attack.

It is not always easy to guard against such dishonesty, though at the outset it may help to make a firm but diplomatic statement that any manipulation will mean immediate withdrawal. Fortunately, once their suspicions are aroused, mediators are usually in a position to consult with their own head-quarters and/or other concerned and knowledgeable persons on the spot. These might be officials of various embassies, representatives of international agencies, the Commonwealth Secretariat, the OAU and other bodies. In fact, such contacts and consultations are a regular feature of mediation. As a mission proceeds, a network of involved people is developed including such as I have just mentioned as well as members of local churches, human rights organisations, academic institutions and so on. Mediators are seldom completely on their own, though they must always guard scrupulously against revealing what has been told them in confidence — if they did so they would never again be trusted and their mission would be ruined. They must also beware of excessive intimacy with or dependence on friends, for example in their own embassy; such intimacy might be taken to imply bias.

The Practice of Mediation

We have seen that would-be mediators have to pass through what might be termed a probationary period, unless of course they have been invited in by the protagonists. However, once they have gained a sufficient measure of acceptance, their work begins to take shape. Although it will obviously change and expand, following the contours of circumstances, it soon becomes possible to identify four aspects of mediation. These are interwoven and overlapping but distinguishable emphases of the unitary task of bringing together those who have been separated by violence.

Building, maintaining and improving communications

By this I mean the mediators' own communications with both groups of protagonists and indeed other involved groups, and — via the mediators — between the protagonists themselves, the second being dependent on the first and both being essential to mediation.

Discussion

There is obviously more to being a messenger than just carrying a message and delivering it like a postman. For one thing, it will often not be written down, but even if so, there is always much to say about the circumstances in which it was sent and the mood of the senders. In addition, it will probably need to be amplified and explained, ambiguities elucidated and so on. The first necessity, therefore, is that mediators should be accepted in this fairly active role (part of what I call active mediation, discussed below) and can in fact communicate with the leaders concerned; communicate in the sense of presenting material that they will listen to and understand and this in turn depends on both having reached a measure of mutual trust and liking. But this is somewhat more in the realm of befriending and will be discussed a little later — for the present I will only repeat that these dimensions of mediation are often inextricably interconnected.

The following incidents illustrate how mediators may attempt to serve as channels of communication between protagonists.

One of the major conferences intended to resolve the Biafran crisis was sponsored in 1968 by the Organisation of African Unity in Addis Ababa under the formidable and remote chairmanship of the late Emperor Haile Selassie. (I had met him once in Ghana, a nobly dignified figure as he stepped from his plane in built-up boots and ostrich-feathered hat; but in a lounge suit resembling a lizard with a squeaky voice — 'Bonjour, Monsieur' he fluted as we were introduced.) Three of us were waiting in the wings and, as usual, keeping in touch with both Nigerian and Biafran delegations. Soon it became obvious that things were not going at all well; both sides made angry statements of seemingly adamantine positions; there was no debate, no give on either side. Everyone was tense and preoccupied; it was difficult to have a reasonable discussion with anyone. The Biafrans were grimly obdurate, pinning their hopes on massive military assistance from France, although they had lost all but three of their larger centres of population. The Nigerians, under the implacable Chief Enahoro, were buoyed up by military successes and convinced that the Biafrans could not long continue organised resistance (in fact they did, for nearly eighteen months). There appeared no hope of compromise and we could see nothing but an indefinite continuation of Biafra's anguish.

Then one evening we had a long talk with Eni Njoku, the chief Biafran delegate. We knew him well, having met him in different parts of Africa, in America and, in happier days, when he was vice-chancellor of the University of Nigeria at Nsukka. He was in a state of muted despair, saying that he had proposals that could break the deadlock, but which he could not make openly because they would appear, wrongly, to imply an abandoment of their position and a loss of nerve. Their only effect, therefore, would be to intensify Nigerian military pressure; the Federal Government would think they had got the Biafrans on the run, and hope they could achieve an all-out victory without any need to compromise.

Whether or not Njoku was right about the possible reception of his proposals, they seemed to us to be reasonable and constructive. They proposed that Biafra (which would even be prepared to relinquish the controversial and inflammatory name) should be accepted as a part of a Nigerian

Union. All they asked for in addition were two measures designed to secure the safety of the people, the great fear then being a repetition of the horrible massacres that had preceded the war. These were, firstly, that they should be allowed some sort of military force; secondly, that they should have a measure of international standing to ensure that any aggression against them would attract international attention and could not be dismissed as a purely 'internal affair'. The military force, Njoku said, could be little more than an armed constabulary, and international standing could be achieved by a seat on the board of one of the UN special agencies or of one of the regional organisations. But since Njoku felt he could not present these proposals without eliciting precisely the opposite effects to what he wished, he asked us to do so instead.

There was no way in which we could present the proposals at the conference, at which we had no official standing, so we decided to return to Lagos. This involved flying up to Rome and then down to Nigeria. I remember the delight of a summer evening in Rome, where we strolled out for a good meal of pasta and a bottle of wine, sandwiched between the heavily steaming heat of Lagos and the wet thin air of the Ethiopian highland.

Gowon was a friendly as ever when we presented, indeed argued, Njoku's case. He promised that the Biafran's ideas would be given consideration, and we left to return to America, where I was then based.

A little later we were told that there had been much discussion of the proposals, but that the hawks had won. They said that nothing new was offered, it was all a trick, a device to gain time. So that, for the time being, was that. But shortly after one of us met the Nigerian ambassador at the UN, who had not heard what had been going on. When he did, he was horrified that the Biafran proposals had been abandoned, maintaining that they did in fact constitute an important new initiative. He hurried back to Lagos to revive the debate. But by this time the military fortunes of the Biafrans had to some extent revived; they no longer wanted the sort of settlement that would have satisfied them when things were going badly.

We had another comparable experience that illustrates the diversity of a mediator's life. Two of us agreed to transport $57,000 in cash (a formidable amount in 1968), which had been raised to help the centres which had been established for starving people driven by war from their homes in Biafra. It was a rather hectic journey — as we spiralled down at night to the Uli air strip, a mere widened roadway, incessant flashes from the battle down below lit up the jungle, and the tracer curled up towards us. Half-way through our journey to deliver the money we had a meeting with Sylvanus Cookey, a trusted lieutenant of Ojukwu. He said the situation was desperate, the federal army was constantly advancing along the main roads (as we discovered, since we had to drive through the jungle to avoid the armoured cars); it was essential that we arrange a meeting to discuss a cease-fire as soon as possible.

As quickly as we could, we flew out on a Red Cross plane to what was then the Spanish island of Fernando Po and thence to Cameroon. My friend went to Lagos to inform the Nigerian Government; I went to London to tell the Commonwealth Secretariat and the British Government, then on to America.

After a few days, however, our hopes were dashed once more. Ojukwu made a fire-eating speech saying that the Biafrans would never yield a square inch of their sacred territory. What did this mean, asked Gowon, who was quite ready to go ahead with the cease-fire; had they really changed their collective mind? The Quakers were asked to contact Biafran representatives in Europe to find out. But no one really knew. Soon, however, came an invitation to return to Biafra along with a number of Biafran representatives who had apparently questioned the wisdom of continuing the war.

I did not go, but my two friends did. On arrival, they were kept incommunicado for five days before being subjected to a tirade by Louis Mbanefo, the Chief Justice, and several others of the Biafran top brass. The main theme was that they would never surrender, and that we should let everyone know that they would accept no compromise. Finally they apologised for speaking so harshly, saying there was no one else to whom they could let off steam. And that, once more, was that. My friends returned puzzled.

The reason soon became clear, however. General de Gaulle had come through with his hoped-for assistance and there had been a massive air-lift of arms from neighbouring Gabon, one of the four African states that had recognised Biafra. The Biafrans decided that, after all, they had a chance; they counter-attacked and recaptured Owerri. This made them bitterly regret the loss of nerve that had induced them to sue for peace. Their behaviour towards us was designed to demonstrate that they had not weakened in their resolve to fight on.

Of course some message carrying has more satisfactory but perhaps less interesting results. For example, we once transmitted a plea for a cease-fire which was agreed to immediatley without the need for any discussion or argument. But the ultimate success of efforts to act as a channel of communication comes when the protagonists themselves take over, no longer needing the intervention of mediators.

Providing information

This means attempting to be aware of facts needed to establish reasonable policies and so as not to be misled by rumour, misinformation or prejudice; peace and negotiation are jeopardised more by ignorance than by truth, however unpalatable. Providing information is, of course, also an aspect of communication, especially because the manner of transmission and the quality of the relationship determines whether it will be heard or understood.

Discussion

Mediators are often in a good position to supply important information for the initiation of moves towards peace — and for keeping them moving. Much of this information tends to be negative, refutations of statements made by each side about the other, such as the following: 'We want a negotiated settlement, but it's no good, because our enemies are set on a military solution'. Mediators moving between the sides may be able to provide evidence that each side's interpretation of the other's intentions is faulty.

But in fact, any remarks about the other side must be made with caution. Both, while not being so crass as to ask obviously military questions, will be eager to glean information of tactical or strategic relevance; mediators hoping to promote peace may unintentionally satisfy their curiosity. If, for example, they hope to prove the sincerity of peace feelers by mentioning the other side's low morale and fear of losing, the enemy might instead take it as an incentive to attack.

But of course the opposite would also be true; if morale was high when the peace feeler was floated, it might be a reason to consider negotiation. However, every case is likely to be different and would need consideration on its own merits, and generally mediators do well to steer away from all military matters which are often subject, especially to the uninitiated, to contradictory interpretations. If, for example, mediators become aware that conscription is being introduced or extended it could imply either a determination to wage war more fiercely, or that losses were great and the bottom of the man-power barrel was being scraped.

One other sort of dilemma over military matters is moral rather than pseudo-psychological. Mediators may, in their travels or conversations, learn of preparations for an offensive in a particular area where great loss of life will inevitably be sustained. Should they give any warning? I think probably not. Firstly, they may be wrong and so sacrifice their impartiality for nothing. Secondly, even if they are right, the people to whom they give the facts would never again trust them as mediators — they would have shown that they were informers. But again there are different scales of violence. Nuclear or some other catastrophic attack should no doubt be prevented by any means possible.

Mediators are on clearer grounds in speaking of individual opinions. Most leaders, in attempting to evaluate the seriousness of peace proposals made by their opposite numbers, will want to know what various people have said about them, and mediators should be able to feel free to tell them as much as they know. They can give the context, possibly including the tone of voice and expression, in which comments reported in the media were made, and give details of happenings from personal experience or the often unavailable international press, which were relevant to the search for peace. In general, they can supply a full, objective and balanced account of crucial events rather than the frequently fragmentary details on which policies are precariously based.

They can be useful in other respects. For example, during the Nigerian civil war, the Biafrans, until a colleage convinced them to the contrary, were dubious about accepting the Commonwealth Secretariat as a mediating body because, being based in London, they assumed it must share the pro-Federal Nigerian views of the British government. In this instance and that of the Zimbabwe war, in which one side lacked the advantages of a foreign ministry and full intelligence services, there was always the danger of fatally faulty judgements. Mediators, free to travel around the world, can often fill a gap in information needed to develop sound policies for settling a conflict.

Befriending

This refers to the character of the relationship between mediators and those with whom they are dealing. They come essentially as friends, drawn by concern for the suffering of all concerned in the struggle, including the mental anguish of those in power. They play a different part from that of civil servant, diplomat or consultant; they come in a spirit of goodwill to do whatever they can to help the victims of the conflict to escape from the trap of violence. To the extent that their unconditional goodwill is accepted, the relationship of the mediators with leaders and other responsible officials may somewhat diminish the psychological tensions and the possibility of compulsive and unconstructive action.

Discussions

The first and most necessary step towards befriending harrassed leaders (or anyone else, for that matter) is to think of them with respect and liking. But how is this possible when some of them may have a most unattractive reputation for, for example, cruelty and violence?

I have struggled with myself before going to meet a leader whose forces have recently committed an act of great barbarity. I felt an impulse to assuage my own distress by accusing him, but knew that to do so would impair my usually good contact with him. But I also knew that simply suppressing my emotions was not enough; my feelings would affect him even if disguised. So I made an effort to calm myself, practising what I had been taught as a child — count ten (in this case much more!) before speaking in anger. This helped me to realise what I had really known all along, that a general at the base could have little direct control of his troops on the front line. Beyond this, however, I realised — and have realised in many other instances — how people may be driven by circumstances, and that I had no cause to reprobate in others what I would have done or felt in their place.

Speaking in general, I then move on to consider the positive things about the person concerned, warmth, courage, sincerity, and indeed about the basic strengths of human nature. Finally I know that s/he is someone just like myself, that we are both in our different ways, up against the same fundamental problems, needing each other's help, respect and compassion and only damaged by each other's contempt or anger.

Understanding this, I break the shell of preoccupation with my own feelings and the equally cramping shell of preconception I had built around this person, crediting (or more properly discrediting!) her/him with unpleasing qualities that might not really exist and neglecting inner richness that might.

It then becomes possible to do what is one of the bases of building a human relationship; to listen and give full attention to the person I have come to see. Once we consciously try to do this, we realise how little we usually hear and give. We may hear the words our friend speaks but we do not reflect on or remember them for more than a very short while. But when the mind is relatively clear and uncluttered by distracting preoccupations, we are free to devote a much higher proportion of our attention to another. This means to be really aware of her/him; it means to open ourselves, to make ourselves available, in a sense to embrace. This is always felt by the other as somehow reassuring and encouraging, but only to the extent that it is done with genuine sincerity.

The listening element of attention giving is crucial. Everyone knows that listening, not necessarily profoundly but just letting people talk, is helpful to anyone in trouble. But to listen with real attention often, and unexpectedly, helps them to gain real insight into themselves.

Although this type of listening requires effort, it is different from the effort needed to hear a very quiet speaker. The effort is to maintain attention, to cut the distractions from one's own mind, and to open the hearing wide to include not only the words but the tone in which they are spoken and all other sounds within earshot.

I would not claim that this approach to befriending will lead always to an intimate relationship, rather to one of confidence and goodwill in which there is also a measure of warm feeling.

Since mediators, though deeply involved in the total situation, are separate from the quarrels, rivalries, clan and tribal antipathies and jealousies that often surface in times of stress, they may be able to provide some respite and relaxation from tension. This relaxation of the pressure of strain, of the threatened ego's quest for self-justification, tends to release the inherent capacity for sound and compassionate judgement upon which depend wise and humane decisions.

In conclusion I should explain, and perhaps excuse, the somewhat personal manner in which befriending has been discussed. I have done so because befriending another human being is a particularly individual matter. I have not pretended to give a prescription for what ought to be done, only an example of what one individual has found helpful.

Active mediation

I have coined this term to describe (inadequately) what might be thought of as the more specifically diplomatic activity of mediators. It is not their job, of course, to attempt persuasion or to promote particular approaches to the resolution of a conflict. On the other hand, they do not just passively and impersonally impart information and pass messages; they are not civil servants whose job it is to ensure that their political masters are aware of all the facts necessary for them to decide on wise policies, but who have no part in those decisions. Mediators, of course, attempt to do these things, but they do so with a specific purpose: to remove obstacles on the path to peace, and they argue strongly against the misunderstandings and preconceptions that strengthen those obstacles.

In order to illustrate this aspect of mediation, and also to a considerable extent the three others that have already been discussed, I have transcribed and suitably edited and modified to make identification impossible even by those concerned, since I have changed sequences, combined situations and fictionalised some details, a number of discussions between a head of state, prime minister or other high official, or a guerilla leader (P) and a mediator or mediators (M).

Discussion

M. I have just been to the other side, where I had a long talk with the head of the military government, General X.
P. What did he say?
M. He said he hoped it would be possible to find a way of bringing the war to an end.
P. What a hypocrite! If he really hopes that, why does he go on bombing our cities; why has he launched a new offensive in the East?
M. He doesn't really strike me as a hypocrite. In fact I felt he was a decent and honest man.
P. (*grunts*)
M. What he says is that he can't negotiate from a position of military inferiority and so has to keep up the pressure.
P. (*speechifying somewhat*) I will never yield to pressure. We will continue the battle until victory is achieved.

M. Yes, of course. But I'm given to understand that both you and he would prefer a settlement to a fight to the finish. That could only do untold damage to both your countries and cause untold suffering to your people.

P. Well, yes. But what can I do if he pursues this course of brutal aggression except hit him back harder to make him think again?

M. Unfortunately he then feels *he* has to hit you harder still to make *you* think again. So we get a vicious spiral of escalation.

P. You seem to be suggesting that *I* am responsible for the increasing violence. I rather resent that. I've told you often enough that I'm seeking every possible way towards a just settlement.

M. Please don't misunderstand me; I know you are. But I also think General X is too. The trouble is that war is a trap. Once it closes its very hard to get out. As I see it, both you and X are caught. What is sad is that when people get caught, their efforts to escape, like escalating the level of violence so as to be able to negotiate from strength, only trap them more firmly.

P. I suppose I have to admit that.

M. And there's a sort of psychological violence which makes extrication even harder. The longer this process goes on, the greater the reciprocal hatred and suspicion; the more both sides reject peace feelers as tricks.

P. All right. But it doesn't help much just to be told I'm in a trap; if it's true, how the hell do I get out of it?

M. Well, General X several times said that he didn't think you were sincere when you spoke of wanting peace, just as you don't think he's sincere to talk about peace at the same time as he bombs your towns. So the first thing is to do something to demonstrate your sincerity.

P. Such as what?

M. Probably the most convincing thing would be something you have refused to do in the past or for some reason clearly don't want to do.

P. You mean something that would put me at a disadvantage.

M. Yes, that's the whole point. If it did, it would prove your sincerity.

P. Or my weakness or stupidity.

M. That could be avoided. It would depend on what was done, how it was done, and how it was presented to the other side.

P. Could you help?

M. Yes, of course, I would be glad to go over to see General X and explain, but of course it would be up to you to decide what to do — an exchange of wounded prisoners, opening up a corridor for relief trucks to the enclave, inviting Amnesty International to inspect your POW camps, no more bombing of civilian targets — something like that.

P. That's possible, I suppose, but I can't see that any move towards peace might not be seen as a sign of weakness. I've got him on the run, X would think, so I'll hit him harder and push him further.

M. That could be a risk, but I don't think a big one. My sense of it is that he would be relieved and so would most of his cabinet except perhaps Y, who doesn't seem to be as powerful as he was. However, you could demonstrate both your sincerity and your strength by letting it be known that while offering a cease fire or whatever, you were also preparing to take very tough measures if X didn't reciprocate, or tried to take advantage of you.

P. But I still don't see why it has to be me to take the first step.

M. In fact it doesn't. I had a somewhat similar conversation with General X who said more or less the same things as you. So he might come up with a proposal any day. But this sort of thing is hard to synchronise; in practice someone has to set the ball rolling.

P. I still think it would give an impression of weakness.

M. I really doubt it, especially if you took the precaution we have considered. But I would look at it in the opposite way. To take some risk for the sake of peace would seem to me a sign of strength, of the courage to take a chance.

P. So you admit there could be a risk?

M. Oh, yes, of course; everything you do in war is risky — including doing nothing or making the automatic conventional response. But it's really a question of the odds. In this case you might lose a little if things went wrong. But if things went right you might gain peace. So it could be a worthwhile gamble.

P. It might be.

* * *

P. I hear you have been talking to the Prime Minister A. I would be interested to know what you make of him.

M. Well, he's obviously a very shrewd man, very realistic, I thought.

P. I only know him from his speeches and other statements, and of course from what he does — his unbridled attack on my country and his obvious hatred of me and my people. You might as well call Hitler shrewd and realistic.

M. (*laughs*) That's going a bit far, I think. As for his speeches, however, you know the sort of thing a war leader is expected to say, all blood and glory and victory over our bestial enemies, that sort of thing. If I may say so without offence, you are pretty good at it yourself. And on that evidence, A has formed the same sort of opinion about you as you have of him.

P. Absurd. Everybody knows I hate war and wish for nothing personally but to live in peace with my wife and children.

M. In fact, so does A. He has a lovely family and I even had supper with his mother, a sweet old lady.

P. Of course I knew he was married, but I assumed it was just one of those formal arrangements.

M. Far from it.

P. But in a way that makes me see him in an even worse light. I simply can't understand how a man who loves his family can commit such atrocities, wiping out hundreds of other loving families. It doesn't hang together, somehow.

M now finds himself in a dilemma, he is half tempted to tell P that A has made the same comment about him, but fears there might be an explosion of rage from the affronted ego that will blow their relationship to pieces. So he decides on a safer course at present, but hopes that some day he may be able to drive home the mirror image lesson that in almost every *bad* respect P and A view each other in a similar way.

M. Well, the exigencies of war force everyone to do things they never expected to do. I'm sure you and A, when you took office, never imagined the sorts of expediences to which you have been driven.

P. Yes. That's so, but of course he, as the aggressor, must bear the whole responsibility for what has happened since.

M swiftly considers whether to raise the philosophical issue of who is and who is not the aggressor. It was true (perhaps) that A's forces fired the first shots. But was not the provocation by P's people that led to the attack, an earlier act of aggression? And why had they offered this provocation? Surely it was because... and so on to the dawn of history or, to a fundamentalist Christian, the incident in the garden of Eden that started all the trouble. If so, it would seem in many cases to be senseless to talk of one party as being the guilty one; both are bound together by the same chain of causation. However, the rulers of nations at war demand that their foe be labelled 'aggressor', and themselves the innocent victims of aggression. Once again M doesn't feel it wise to make a frontal attack on this facet of P's ego. On the other hand, the way forward to negotiations is seriously blocked if the protagonists see each as implacably hostile and negative. But perhaps something else could be said to weaken P's fixed idea of A as a conniving, evil and violent sub-human.

M. Yes. But I think it's worth remembering that he inherited a very difficult situation. The combination of domestic and international pressures pushed him inexorably towards war.

P. You're making excuses for him.

M. No, I'm not — oh, I suppose in a way I am. But I think public figures can't always be held completely responsible for their actions. A leader's decision — but you know this much better than me — is usually the end point of much discussion and many compromises. But he is the one who carries the can and he's the one with whom one has to deal. So it's a good thing to know what he's like, that he's not an entirely self-sufficient, self-existent force, but a pretty able human being having some decent impulses, trying to make sense out of the conflicting demands on him and to do what appears to be the best possible thing in the circumstances.

P. You're not trying to make me like him, are you?

M. No. But I'm suggesting that it would be a good thing to keep an open mind about him, not to reject the idea that he could be a more reasonable person to deal with than you seem to think.

P. (*grunts sceptically*)

M. Anyway, the fact remains that unless you go on battering each other to pieces, you will eventually have to get together and sort out the terms of a settlement. Its your shared problem and you somehow have to solve it together.

* * *

P. You have several times talked about my having dealings with my enemies, or even having a relationship with them.

M. Yes.

P. The only way I want to deal with them is by beating hell out of them till they want to cry quits, and the only relationship I intend to have is to dictate my terms to them. I don't want any of this lovey-dovey crap.

M. I know you feel very bitter about what they have done, but when I talk about relationships I don't mean something you should try to establish. I mean that, like it or not, it's something that exists. It's a fact. You are both locked into a relationship, a very bad one certainly, because you are both involved in the same problem. In fact you are involved in it so much and it is so difficult that you have gone to war over it. But war *is* a relationship. It's just as much a relationship as when you were arguing about it at the UN and had a political relationship, exchanging ambassadors and so on, with them.

P. So what. I don't see where this twaddle is getting us.

M. Sorry if I'm irritating you. I'm just suggesting that this whole disastrous situation exists because of a common problem that relates you to each other. I don't see how you can solve it except through the relationship which exists *de facto*. In some way you have to find out how to cooperate.

P. Are you crazy. Me cooperate with this bastard W? No, I'll beat his rotten army to pulp and then hang him. That'll solve the problem.

M. If you say so. But I understood when we first talked that you were interested in mediation because you felt that to go for a purely military solution would be too costly. Also that it wouldn't actually be a solution, because you would still be left with a sullen and rebellious population who would continue the conflict by other means and eventually, perhaps, by another armed struggle. I am simply suggesting that if you want to resolve the conflict in a way that sticks, you will have to do it somehow in conjunction with W. But if you do intend to settle the whole business by crushing them militarily, you don't need a mediator. So just tell me and I'll leave.

P. OK, OK. Now assuming you are right, what's the next step?

M. To start with you could send him a message through me; I expect to see him next month.

P. Right. Just tell him to get lost.

M. (*laughs*) If he did you would have to deal with Z who is even more difficult.

P. Seriously, I'm not sure what I want to convey to him. I have told him often enough that I'll talk, but he hasn't responded, except to repeat his absurd proposals.

M. It must be an irritating deadlock for you.

P. It certainly is. But how the devil to break it?

M. It seems to me that these rather formal public announcements often don't fully represent a government's position; they are made for other reasons than just negotiation. They are intended to satisfy the opposition in one's own country and to encourage wavering supporters, to impress the world with one's determination, and so on. But usually behind the rhetoric there is some scope for flexibility.

P. Quite right. There are one or two points on which we could bend a little. But how can we present them without losing face, giving the impression of climbing down?

M. They don't have to be made officially. We could deliver a spoken message that couldn't be used against you because you could dissociate yourself from it if necessary. If you agree, we could possibly suggest, on our own account perhaps, that you might be prepared to relax your stand on some issues. We could add that you would only be ready to do so if they were prepared to reciprocate, a sort of tit-for-tat arrangement.

P. Do you have any ideas on where I should be prepared to bend?

M. No, we don't. We can't suggest what is best for your country, only how to remove obstacles to achieving it.

P. That makes sense.

M. We would hope that this might mark the beginning of a process that really might end in fruitful cooperation.

P. And I suppose this relationship you're so keen on.

* * *

P. This business about the island is getting very worrying.

M. It must be. Do you think Exia really intends to invade?

P. I'm afraid it really looks likely. I've reinforced the local garrison. But the way President F is talking, that probably won't deter them. And that means war; God knows where it will stop.

M. Is there no alternative?

P. I don't think so. We obviously can't yield on any issue affecting our territorial integrity; that's a matter of essential national principle.

M. I'm a bit cautious about statements like that. In their book, *Getting to Yes*, Fisher, who is a friend of mine and Ury say it's important to keep position, roughly what you refer to as principle, separate from interest, and to emphasise interest.

P. I don't see what you are getting at. My ancestors annexed the Island three centuries ago. It's obviously part of our interest to keep control of it and maintain our dominion intact.

M. Is it, though? Everyone acknowledges it has no strategic or economic value. The people are linguistically and culturally closer to Exia than to you, and have been a constant headache to your governments from the beginning. One could argue that it would actually be in the national interest to get rid of this worthless Island and its unruly inhabitants; that the *principle* of hanging on to it is not in your *interest*.

P. That's absurd. If I were to tamely let go of the Island, my government would fall and the Exians and every other potential aggressor in the region would think they could bully and blackmail us.

M. Yes. I see that. But what you are saying is that you are hanging on to a position or principle less because of the advantage it brings or interest it serves, than because of disadvantages to your vital interests that might follow from discarding it.

P. (*reluctantly*) There may be something in that.

M. Please don't be offended if I take the argument a little farther. If, at this juncture, you stick to your principle of territorial sovereignty and are forced into war, others of your interests will undoubtedly suffer. The economy will certainly be harmed, many of your young men will be maimed or killed — how many lives, I wonder, is it proper to sacrifice for a principle — and above all there is a chance that you might lose the war, one or other of you must; then everything would be lost — the Island, the young men who fought in vain, the good repute of your administration; nothing would survive but the principle that brought such disaster.

P. You are certainly frank. My predecessors would have had you shot for talking like that. But it sickens me, too, when I remember what might happen to our boys. What can I do, though? We are trapped in a situation where I can't see any way of avoiding war, that is, if the Exians go on with this mad venture.

M. Well, I'm not sure they want to. I have an idea that President F may feel as trapped as you do. Suppose he has been whipping up feelings about the Island for domestic political purposes and is horrified to realise what he has let himself in for now that he has roused the tiger of militaristic chauvinism.

P. (*sarcastically*) My heart bleeds for the poor fellow.

M. I hope to be able to find out more about it next week when I go to Exia. Anyway, if I'm right that he would like a let-out, a bit of quiet diplomacy might provide you both with an honourable solution to what may be a joint problem. I mean one which would bring you credit for restraint and wisdom, while also avoiding all dangers of abandoning principles without safeguarding interests.

P. What sort of solution are you talking about?

M. The details would be up to you. However, if you both decide to modify or withdraw from an inflexible position — his being that he must have the Island, yours being that he musn't — and instead consider your common interests — avoiding the ravages of war — it shouldn't be too difficult to find one. For example, you might, on the accepted and respected principle —

P. Ha! I thought you rejected principles.

M. (*laughs*) Not in every case — of self-determination, offer to hand over the Island to UN trusteeship; or lease it to Exia for so many years, after which a referendum would decide whether it returned to your rule, or to the Exians, or became independent.

P. But the population is not more than ten thousand.

M. The same in some of the South Pacific nations. But the point I'm making is that this type of solution would have the great advantage for you of avoiding confrontation without giving in to Exia, and at the same time of making a generous, and altruistic international gesture that would be widely appreciated. And for President F it would have the advantage of changing the status of the Island in a way that would satisfy his most carping critics, without war. And I'm sure the regional organisation would be greatly relieved and do whatever possible to help.

P. I still wonder how my people would respond to what the opposition would certainly represent as a betrayal.

M. Surely with relief. They don't really want war, do they?

P. (*shakes his head*).

★ ★ ★

M. The other side have suggested that it might be a helpful move to have a temporary cease-fire in the southern sector.

P. Why?

M. It might reduce tensions to a point where negotiations seemed possible.

P. But they know, the world knows, that we are ready to negotiate at any time.

M. I'm afraid they don't believe this.

P. Why? Didn't I say so at the General Assembly only three weeks ago?

M. Yes, indeed. However, in the rather tense atmosphere of war, what people say counts for much less than what they do. In fact you may remember that their leader made a very similar statement.

P. Oh, him. No one believes a word he says.

M. Forgive me, but that is what he said about you.

P. (*splutters angrily*)

M. But you see that the fact that you both dislike and mistrust each other makes it necessary, if you are really interested in a negotiated peace, that you make some practical demonstration of good faith.

P. Very well, let them cease their aggression in the southern sector and we will follow suit.

M. That would be as unacceptable to them as it would be to you. You would both fear that the other would take advantage of you.

P. Yes, I suppose so. If there were to be a cease-fire it would have to be simultaneous and bilateral. But I must say, the whole idea doesn't attract me.

M. Why?

P. How would I know they wouldn't use the opoportunity to consolidate their positions, and to bring up more troops and supplies?

M. It's possible, but there might be a way of avoiding that danger.

P. What do you mean?

M. To bring in a third-party monitoring force — the UN, the Commonwealth, the OAU, for example.

P. Oh, no. My cabinet wouldn't permit any internationalisation of the conflict.

M. I'm afraid that if you took that line, the other side would assume you simply intended to use the cease-fire to gain the advantage you fear they would seek. In that case, if they hadn't already started, they would certainly strengthen their positions and reinforce their troops. The cease-fire would be something of a farce, unstable and temporary.

P. So the whole idea is no good.

M. No, no. If you really hope to reach a negotiated settlement as soon as possible, the other side's proposal for a cease-fire is a good one. If honestly put into force it would provide a cooling-off period during which bloodshed was greatly reduced — and the more the killing the more the unreason of war fever — and preparations for negotiations pursued.

P. But suppose the whole thing is a trick? Suppose they are just making what seems like an attractive offer hoping I'll either reject it, in which case they win a propaganda point, or I accept it, in which case they use it as I have suggested. I just don't trust them.

M. In our opinion they made the offer in good faith, and we believe that if you turned it down you would lose an opportunity that might not recur for a long time. But of course you would be right to take whatever steps you felt necessary to preserve the cease-fire intact.

P. You mean the monitoring arrangement?

M. Yes.

P. How would it be worked?

M. I don't know much about that sort of thing except that it is done, but I could put you in touch with people who do.

★ ★ ★

P. I find it very puzzling. You say that Q wants to edge towards negotiation, but if so, why doesn't he make some sort of answer to the terms I have suggested? I don't expect him to agree to all of them, at least not right away. But complete silence seems to me tantamount to rejection.

M. It could be interpreted that way, but President Q told us only last week that he couldn't find a satisfactory way to answer. Several of his advisers told me the same story independently — we don't believe they were all having us on.

P. But why? What's so difficult?

M. They said your proposals were so unresponsive to what they were demanding that there was nothing to be said. One of them, Q himself I think, put it like this. Suppose a man is sick with pneumonia and you give him a sulfa drug, then you are at least responding, even though a bit inadequately, to his needs: he may be able to persuade you that an antibiotic is a more affective medicine. But if you give him an aspirin, well, that has nothing to do with pneumonia at all and shows you have no understanding of his illness whatsoever.

P. I can't believe my proposals were so irrelevant. I really can't understand what Q is up to. If he doesn't like my offer, which I personally think is generous, why doesn't he say so, and state his terms clearly. Then we could get down to business.

M. There are perhaps two things here. They say that they have always made it quite clear what they were fighting for; they have done so in general terms of principle using such words as sovereignty and autonomy. However, they are scared of expressing the general in terms of the specific — frontier demarcations, relations within the regional economic organisation — things like that.

P. Why be scared of that?

M. They have told me, and asked me to convey to you, that they are not pressing for all the territory you have assumed they claim; they would not expect the autonomy of the northern islands. But they don't want to make this public until a settlement is in sight as their people might feel short-changed — but if a reasonable agreement were in the offing they would feel satisfied.

P. I think it's all very muddled and confusing. I don't see what I can do.

M. What they would like you to do is to come up with a whole new set of proposals, something they could feel was more like the sulpha drugs or even, preferably, penicillin.

P. They must realise that would be politically impossible, out of the question. And that's why I think Q keeps stalling on negotiations, making ridiculous excuses. I'm convinced, and my intelligence people have some evidence, that they are going to go for the military solution, which means that I shall have to also.

M. We agree that it's very confusing. If we were you, we would probably draw the same conclusions. But knowing President Q and a lot of his people we find it hard to disbelieve them completely. They say they are also confused. They say they can't understand why, if you want to negotiate, you don't make an offer you can both negotiate and haggle over. That makes *them* think that *you* intend to go for a military solution.

P. But they haven't got the slightest evidence that could suggest that.

M. Once the suspicion is there, very little evidence is needed by them or by you. Any tough speech, any troop movements, any arms purchases, provides proof.

P. Then what's to be done?

M. We think Q is mistaken not to present terms, but we gather his difficulties are compounded by a disunited cabinet. Anyhow, we can urge him to make some response. It might be helpful if you could send a message.

P. I'll think about it.

M. We don't necessarily mean a direct message, but a statement in a speech, preferably one of which I could warn them in advance, saying something less implacable than usual. You might hint, for example, that you would welcome talks if they would respond to your overtures.

P. I'll think about it.

* * *

P. I really don't understand you people. You say you don't get any profit from all this travelling around which must often be tiresome and difficult. Why do you do it?

M. (*expressing views which are by no means necessarily shared by all mediators but which illustrate the beliefs and motivations that affect some of them*) We feel very strongly over all the suffering brought about by violence — the destruction of lives and homes and the mental anguish of everyone involved, especially those who, like you, carry such awesome responsibilities.

P. Do you think it's wrong to use violence? What else could we have done in our circumstances?

M. Yes, we do feel war is wrong, but the world being as it is, it's impossible to blame people for resorting to it. What we would hope to do is to help them discover a way of disentangling themselves from it, to find an alternative way of settling their differences.

P. Do you mean war is against the will of God, or something like that?

M. I personally don't argue that way; it would seem to imply that people who seek peaceful solutions are somehow morally superior to those who don't. But I believe we resort to violence, all of us in one way or another, because we have a faulty view of human nature.

P. How?

M. We feel we are self-sufficient and independent entities, but we aren't. Everything we do and think is the product of forces — other persons, history — acting on us. And everything we do and think is a comparable force affecting other people and events. Like sub-atomic particles in a field of force, we are part of a system, elements that are constantly interacting and being affected by each other with inherently unpredictable outcomes.

P. I can see that. But what has it to do with war and violence.

M. This. If we think of human beings, ourselves, as separate entities, we essentially feel we can order our affairs without reference to others, hence the obsession with our own interests, with what is right for *me.* We expand this principle to the groups we belong to, or through which we operate, the family, the state, whatever. Basically, although the superficial causes of wars vary enormously, the underlying causes derive from this principle. One nation or group attacks another because it feels that its interest will be served thereby, or that if it does not they will be harmed; or for the same reasons it behaves in such a way, oppressively for example, that causes others to attack it. What both sides fail to realise is that hardly ever, except perhaps sometimes briefly, do they get from war what they hoped to achieve.

P. If I really thought that I'd have to resign, wouldn't I?

M. Well, what I believe we all have to do, whoever we are, is to realise that we aren't isolated. We do something, which may be on a vast scale like declaring war, or on a minute one like leaving an unrewarding job, believing that these are isolated actions which will change one aspect of life thus eradicating a nagging problem without which everything else will be fine. But nothing will ever be the same again. The war will create new problems, the unrewarding job will be followed by the misery of unemployment.

P. That's a very pessimistic view; what's the point of doing anything?

M. It's this. If we fully realise how intimately we are all connected, even with our greatest enemies, and see that our fates are bound together, we can look for ways of solving our problems *together.* But if we think of ourselves as lonely entities struggling with what we feel to be an alien and malign force, things get more and more out of control; they go from bad to worse.

P. You mean that if we act as though humanity is one and don't just concentrate on one small piece of it, the world will be a better place?

M. Precisely. That's why I'm against violent solutions.

P. But I don't see how it helps me to find a peaceful way out of our present violent conflict.

M. I don't either, but let me say this: most of your difficulties with R come from your deep distrust of each other. When you feel like that you (I mean both of you, naturally) see unsurmountable snags to every possible solution. But if you could somehow feel differently about him....

P. Please don't preach to me about loving him.

M. I wouldn't dream of it. I would say however that people in these situations of war come to see each other somewhat unrealistically. All I would hope is that they come to see each other realistically instead. They are bound to each other by the closest ties except love —

they are trying to kill each other. It is only by working together that they can both escape from this awful symbiosis. They may of course find this very hard unless they also remember that they are linked by their common humanity, which joins them at a more fundamental level than that which separates them.

P. Well, I don't know about all that. You make it sound very metaphysical.

M. I'm sorry. I'm really trying to say something very practical. You and R, as I know well, both feel the same about extricating your countries honourably from this struggle in which you are hurting each other so badly. If you can realise that you have the same objective, you will find it easier to cooperate to reach it — which you will have to do some day if you are not to annihilate each other. I believe that rather than a frantic search for peace formulae what is needed is a changed attitude towards each other. Develop that and the practical issues will easily be settled.

* * *

M. I've just come back from a visit to the other side.

P. I would be interested to hear about it.

M. The experience which is most on my mind was very distressing. I was taken to a market-place where 128 women and babies had been killed by a single bomb, cut to pieces.

P. I find that deeply distressing too. After all, although they are rebels I feel they are my people and I grieve at their death. The only thing I can say is that such ghastly events will teach them a lesson that may lead to the end of the war.

M. What lesson?

P. That rebellion doesn't pay, it leads to tragedy.

M. And. . . ?

P. Well, they should lay down their arms.

M. Please forgive me for contradicting you, but the effect of this bombing is quite the opposite. What they say is that it proves everything their propaganda has been saying about genocide. . .

P. (*interrupting*) But they can't believe that one isolated and most unfortunate incident, probably caused by the pilot's lack of experience, is proof of something so unthinkable.

M. But they do. I think if I may say so, that it is very hard for anyone who hasn't been there to imagine the desperation of a beleaguered people. They see the threat of malevolence everywhere. So what they are saying is this: we now see that he means to kill us all, why else should he destroy women and children who have nothng to do with the war? We might as well go on fighting rather than just wait to be butchered; and who knows, there may always be a miracle.

P. (*distressed*) But I have made countless broadcasts saying that as soon as they surrender there will be a complete amnesty for everyone, that there is nothing to fear.

M. I know, but in these situations actions speak louder than words.

P. (*looks very sad, but says nothing*)

M. That's the awful thing about war. Once is begins, horrible things happen. Everyone is guilty and, in another sense, nobody.

* * *

P. We were very disappointed at the failure of the peace conference.

M. Why do you think it was unsuccessful?

P. They just shouted slogans at us, refused to discuss our proposals sensibly. There was no negotiation at all. We did our best and are very discouraged; we don't see the way forward at all.

M. Perhaps it was the wrong sort of meeting.

P. Well, what would you suggest?

M. It may have been too public. They were not only shouting these slogans at your people, but at their own people and at the world's press. They may have felt, in fact they told us, that it wasn't an atmosphere in which they felt they could discuss complicated details and so felt all they could do was to state their case as clearly and firmly as they could.

P. And in consequence foolishly lose a chance of ending this wretched business.

M. I think we have to take into account the state of their internal affairs. As you know, they depend on the collaboration of the opposition to hold things together and the opposition are if anything more extreme than the government. I'm convinced that the government really do want a settlement but are afraid that a long-drawn-out negotiation, in which inevitably there is some accommodation on both sides, could make things very difficult for them at home.

P. So the whole thing was a farce?

M. Not exactly. They made their point as toughly as they could, which was useful domestically, and there was just a chance that something more might have come out of it.

P. I don't see how.

M. Nor do I, but people tend to hope for miracles.

P. You may be right about all this, but I don't see how it helps us to move forward. I don't propose to set up more conferences just to improve their home standing. What else can we do?

M. When the dust has settled a bit, it might be worthwhile having another meeting, but a quite different sort of meeting.

P. What sort?

M. An entirely secret and unpublicised one — tightest security, no press, no communiqués.

P. I don't see how this could be done. Surely everyone would be aware of a bevy of leading figures converging on some spot.

M. I'm not saying it would be easy, but I was going to suggest that in the first place the participants might be second-level people, the senior officials rather than the ministers, who might not be so noticeable. And they might be better from another angle, they might not feel so pressed to make *political* points and so be better able to get on with the nitty-gritty business of detailed negotiations.

P. Yes, that's right. Also I might add rather cynically that if they make a real cock-up of things, the top leadership will be less closely implicated. Yes, I like it. Could you help?

M. Perhaps. We might be able to arrange a meeting of this sort, but one at a higher level and on a larger scale would be beyond the resources of a non-official organisation.

P. That would, I hope, come later, after this get-together had cleared away some of the obstacles.

M. Yes. The trouble about the last meeting was that there was really no preparation; you just jumped into the main issues before you were ready or had the minimum of mutual understanding.

P. Then there is the question of who should chair the

meeting, or indeed whether we would need a chairman.

M. I think it would be a good thing. Obviously it can't be anyone involved in the conflict; that would inevitably suggest bias, but I think it would be important to have someone respected by both parties who could keep a constructive and organised discussion moving and prevent it from degenerating into a slanging match or getting bogged down in irrelevancy.

P. I agree. Who could we get?

M. Perhaps someone like the president of the Regional UN Organisation?

P. Not him; he's known to sympathise with them. What about one of you?

M. We could perhaps find someone whom we could then suggest to you for approval.

P. Fine. So could you go ahead with arrangements?

M. Gladly. First of all, of course, I shall have to go over to the other side and put the idea to them.

* * *

M. When I talked with Colonel F last week it seemed to me that there was very little separating your position from his.

P. That's surprising. How so?

M. He says that now the only real issue between him and you is the G — corridor and that if you would agree to internationalise it, place it under a UN mandate perhaps, he would give up his claim to it, and of course withdraw his troops.

P. (*angrily*) *His* claim? Ridiculous. It's our territory.

M. Well, as you know, of course, F claims it too, and this would seem a suitable compromise. After all, it's only a few square kilometres of semi-desert inhabited seasonally be a handful of nomads. Infinitely more people would die if both sides continued struggling to occupy it.

P. It's a matter of national honour, something about which we will never compromise. I'm sorry that you've been influenced by their propaganda. I had counted on you to see the justice of our cause, or at least to be impartial.

M realises that he has stepped out of the mediator's role by making a policy suggestion, especially one favouring the enemy's proposal. If he had been asked, it would have been legitimate for him to give his opinion that the saving of life would have been well worth the loss of control over a small area of no strategic or economic importance. As it is, he can only apologise.

M. I'm sorry. But you know we only work out of concern for the suffering caused by conflict and sometimes fail to take proper account of national policy and aspirations. But we are always glad to be put right. And I can assure you that what I just said wasn't influenced by anything Colonel F told me; it was my own bad idea.

P nods forgiveness, which is lucky for M, who had really spoken out of turn. Nevertheless, M had a valid point. Here was a suggestion for a compromise which, face, national pride and ego apart, was perfectly reasonable. It would save precious lives and much misery, no valuable territory would be lost, while the few nomads, if they cared at all under whose national sovereignty they lived, would probably be better off. But his approach should have been cautious, gradual and indirect. He should have tried to steer the discussion so that P began to talk about F's suggestion. M could have set the stage for a more reflective and objective assessment of it by praising, and with some reason, P's realism, humanity and care for his people; not because P is susceptible to flattery but because, like many leaders, he is tense, needs reassurance as to his worth and is apt, in this state, to react in an angry and extreme way. M should then try to start a more relaxed and general conversation in which P might say for himself what he rejected when told by someone else.

Evaluation

What does it all amount to? People who have tried to mediate must always ask themselves whether they have been wasting their time. By the nature of things, anonymous private mediators are not going to be able to bring off dramatic coups. Even if they have made a great contribution to the changed understanding on which a settlement depends, they will not be the ones actually to engineer it. That happens in the public domain such as the UN, the Commonwealth Secretariat, the OAU or a powerful third-party government any of which will have the necessary resources and the technical administrative skills such as were needed, for example, to mount and conduct the Lancaster House Conference that brought the Zimbabwe war to an end. In any case, it would not be appropriate, and might adversely affect their future usefulness, to bring into the open people whose work depends on their invisibility, and it doesn't often happen; in my twenty years' experience, our activities have only on very rare occasions received attention in the media and then it was but slight. I have even wondered if I should write these pages. However, I felt it was legitimate to follow Mike Yarrow's book which I, as a practitioner, found useful, by something which I trust will supplement it. And I have preserved the anonymity of those not mentioned by name in this book, in which the narrative ends in 1970, and have given no details whatsoever of some later mediations.

However, a more important question than the degree of visibility of mediators is whether, seen or unseen, they do any good. Do they contribute at all to peace or do they put themselves and everyone else concerned to considerable effort and expense for nothing? I wish I could give a clear-cut answer, but does one ever know the full effect of anything done with or for other people? Is my wife better for having known me, have I helped my children deal competently and happily with life, are my students wiser because of my teaching, did my efforts in any way improve the quality of existence of the Third World people for whose development I worked? I will never know, just as I will never know whether the money my friend and I took to Biafra utimately did more good than harm.

But this uncertainty doesn't worry me. I try to do what I think right to do, and my Quaker colleagues might feel that this was sufficfient justification, provided I set about the task seriously and carefully, having taken the best available advice. Moreover, if we have any understanding of how things happen, especially in the complex weave of international affairs, we realise that there is never *one* person, *one* group, *one* event to which the final result can be attributed. What, in fact, is a final result? The peace conference, or the settlement, or the resolution (if they occur), are merely commas in a journal that is still going on and will be written until the end of time.

Of one thing, however, we can be certain: mediators *do* have an effect on the total situation. Admittedly, their effect will be very small if they never progress beyond the preliminary stages. However, the closer they get to the main actors and the longer they remain on the stage, the greater their influence on events. They are therefore under an obligation to make that influence a good one. This is likely to be so if they keep their egos in order, and tackle the external issues with informed common sense and sensitivity. At the same time, they should realise that, with all the goodwill and good sense in the world, they may not be able to help having a negative impact on some person or happening. But this, I think, is an acceptable risk. There would perhaps be a greater risk than that if they were *not* involved, their absence would have entailed the loss of important opportunites. I can think of some cases where, had we not been present, a chance of peace-making would have been lost; but whether it was taken by those empowered to do so is another matter.

Mike Yarrow, referring to the difficulty of assessing Quaker private diplomacy, says: 'Evaluation of the effectiveness of any one element. . . in a complicated series of historical processes, is difficult if not impossible. It is like asking for the effectiveness of one thread in a mainsail halyard of many filaments' (p.298).

Nevertheless, although there may be no hard evidence, I believe there are a number of hints of usefulness. Again I quote Yarrow: 'In the case of India and Pakistan just after the [1965] war over Kashmir, the heads of each government used the Quakers to communicate with the other opinions and intentions that could not be publicly stated, particularly with a view to testing the strength of moderate forces working to continue the truce. [It was in fact continued.] In the Nigerian war, the Quaker aim for a negotiated peace was not achieved, but peace by mililtary victory resulted in an amazing degree of magnanimity towards the defeated side. The Quakers may have had a small part in this result, because their efforts were welcomed by certain Nigerian leaders.

'The one objective index of effectiveness available was the fact that the persons involved retained continuing access to the top leadership over a considerable period of time rather than being sent away as importunate meddlers. It is perhaps safe to conclude from this that the Quakers were carrying on an operation which others found useful and not just fooling themselves' (p. 299).

There is little I would like to add to this evaluation, except that well-informed sources in Lagos confirmed to us what Yarrow suggested as our possible contribution to the paradoxically 'peaceful' conclusion to the war. Once the ceasefire was proclaimed the fighting stopped completely. The defeated Biafrans, who had expected to be massacred, were taken by their conquerors to feeding centres, loaded onto military trucks and conveyed to hospital if wounded; the soldiers handed over their own rations to the starving people and gave them money. Immediately Biafrans who had been civil servants or diplomats in the Federal Government had their jobs restored; if there were no immediate vacancy for, for example, a former ambassador, he was placed on full pay until one became available. Such a change of heart seemed almost miraculous. Our contribution, if indeed we were not deceiving ourselves, was that we had been continually trying to explain to the Nigerians why the Biafrans felt as they did; that they did not resist so desperately because they were instransigent and filled with destructive hatred, but because, with reason, they were frightened but wanted peace as much as anyone. In addition, as I have described, on two occasions we carried and interpreted messages that could easily have brought a settlement many months before the actual end of the war.

After the end of the Zimbabwe struggle, where we were involved after the period recorded by Yarrow, Walter Martin, who planned and led the execution of the mediation with the greatest possible sensitivity and skill, received appreciative letters from African leaders and others who knew what had been happening. I also met an American diplomat who told me that it was recognised at the UN, where he had been temporarily attached, that the achievement of peace had largely depended on Quaker efforts; as he had no idea that I had been involved, the comment must be considered as completely unbiased.

As for me, having had my family life disrupted countless times, and often suffering inconvenience, loneliness and occasional illness and danger, I still go on because I believe, and have indeed been told, that it may help. This seems to me sufficient reason to continue trying, and sufficient cause to hope that the effort will bring a small measure of good results.

I am not sure, however, that this form of evaluation can be very fruitful. On the wide screen of conflict, any one happening is the product of innumerable converging forces. It would be rash indeed to attribute greater significance to any one of them. It is wiser, perhaps, to consider what mediation is designed to contribute towards, and how far the process as I have tried to describe it, is suitable for the purpose.

Mediation is intended to break down the barriers of suspicion, unreasonable fear, exaggerated hostility, misunderstanding and ignorance that keep protagonists at a greater distance than is warranted by the practical or material grounds of their quarrel. Only when this has to some extent occured will there be an adequate chance of satisfactory negotiations.

Long term private or non-official mediation focuses on building relationships through which mediation can dispel some of the misconceptions, fixed ideas and irrational dread and hatred that develop all too easily in times of violence. It does so through the quadruple approach of communication, providing information, befriending and active mediation that has been described. This approach, if properly used, should both promote a more genuinely realistic understanding of the situation and diminish the distortions of ego compulsion.

It would be absurd to claim that diplomats, UN officials and negotiators representing various governments and international agencies do not, to a considerable extent do most of the same things; if they did not, they would have scant respect.

Mediators, however, have no other role that could interfere with their fundamental psychological, or it would be more correct to say human, task. They are tied by no policy, they have no other allegiance, they are entirely devoted to working on the mental obstacles to peace, believing that if these can be diminished so will be the material ones.

Why then, we may ask, is this form of mediation so insufficiently developed and employed? It is surely because we do not really understand the roots of conflict, seeing it primarily as an objective state of affairs and not as the states of mind that led to, and subsequently sustained and exaggerated that state of affairs. Consequently our approach to conflict resolution is confused and inefficient. We really know very little about it and after hundreds of years of diplomacy which have admittedly produced many brilliant practitioners, have little scientific understanding of it.

Our chief fault is failure to recognise that conflict is often largely in the mind and to that extent must be dealt with on that level; and that even when it is less so, as in the case of political oppression or economic exploitation, emotional factors exacerbate what is already serious. Consequently we have not developed good methods for dealing with it.

I believe from my own experience that the type of mediation I have tried to define represents a short, wavering step in the right direction. This would seem to be borne out by the very tentative evaluation that has so far been possible. I think, therefore, that mediation needs to be paid more careful and serious attention and, in the following chapter, present some proposals about how that might be done. These are comparable, in fact, to those made by Yarrow (pp. 266–7).

Proposal for an International Mediation Centre

This centre should be set up as a non-governmental organisation (NGO) having consultative status with the UN. The first step towards establishing it might be for one of the bodies directly involved or else interested in mediation to convene a working party of concerned individuals and group representatives. If it seemed reasonable to proceed with the project, this group would (probably) suggest broad guidelines for the further development of the centre. It would obviously be premature to attempt to define the size, administrative structure or agenda of this centre; this could only evolve in a precise form after its establishment. Nevertheless, it seems safe to predict that the following functions would form part of its essential activities.

(1) To develop criteria for the desirability and feasibility of the type of mediation discussed in this essay.

(2) To maintain an overview of the global scene in order to identify situations where mediation was or might become desirable.

(3) To compile a register of persons with experience in mediation and having qualifications, such as a language skill, appropriate for mediation in particular regions or circumstances.

(4) To recruit and launch mediation teams when the directors considered it appropriate, and to give them backstopping assistance when they were in the field.

(5) To raise financial resources for its operations, including funds for 'sabbaticals' to free persons in employment to carry out mediation.

(6) To provide any necessary training or preparation relevant to mediation, especially with a view to ensuring a flow of younger people into the work. At present there is virtually no systematic training for mediation. Most mediators, who come from very varied academic and work backgrounds,

have picked up their abilities 'on the job'. It is most important to find and impart better means of preparing women and men for this demanding task.

(7) To carry out research on the field of conflict in general and on mediation and training for mediation in particular.

Bibliographical Note

The literature on mediation is very scanty, but the following short list may be helpful.

Bailey, Sydney D., 'Non-official mediation in disputes; reflections on the Quaker experience', *International Affairs*, 1985. A fairly short but very informative article which puts the subject into its historical and institutional context.

Bolling, Landrum, 'Quaker work in the Middle East following the June 1967 war', in Maureen R. Berman and Joseph E. Johnson (eds.), *Unofficial Diplomats*, New York, Columbia University Press, 1977.

Burton, J. W., *Conflict and Communication*, London, Macmillan, 1969.

Curle, Adam, *Making Peace*, London, Tavistock Publications, 1971. Chapter 19, 'Conciliation', gives a short account of mediation.

—, *True Justice: Quaker peace makers and peacemaking*, London, Quaker Home Service, 1981 (1981 Swarthmore Lecture).

Fisher, Roger, and William Ury, *Getting to Yes*, London, Hutchinson, 1983. A book on negotiation rather than mediation,but one containing helpful ideas for mediators — such as that others should be treated *as though* they are helpful and want to try to solve problems rather than as tiresome troublemakers.

Jackson, Elmore, *Middle East Mission*, London and New York, Norton, 1983. A fascinating account of a shuttle between Nasser and Ben Gurion.

Rubin, Jeffrey Z. (ed.), *Dynamics of Third Party Intervention: Kissinger in the Middle East*, New York, Praeger, 1981.

Warren, Roland, 'The conflict system and the change agent', *Journal of Conflict Resolution*, vol. 8, no. 3, 1964. Probably the best account of mediation from the point of view of a social scientist.

Yarrow, C. H. Mike, *Quaker Experiences in International Mediation*, New Haven and London, Yale University Press, 1978. By far the most valuable and comprehensive account of mediation from any point of view.

Young, Oran R., *The Intermediaries: Third Parties in International Crisis,* 1967.